Waiting in Joyful Hope

Daily Reflections for Advent and Christmas 2022–2023

Mary DeTurris Poust

LITURGICAL PRESS

Collegeville, Minnesota

www.litpress.org

D1212146

Nihil Obstat: Rev. Robert Harren, J.C.L., *Censor Deputatus*
Imprimatur: ✠ Most Rev. Donald J. Kettler, J.C.L., D.D., Bishop of St. Cloud, January 27, 2022

Cover design by Monica Bokinskie.
Cover art courtesy of Getty Images.

ISSN: 1550-803X
ISBN: 978-0-8146-6692-0   978-0-8146-6693-7 (ebook)

Introduction

Every now and then, when I need a reminder about the importance of waiting, I pull out a recording of theologian Henri J.M. Nouwen giving a talk on the subject. And although I've heard the recording at least a dozen times, every time I play it, I feel my shoulders lower and my breathing slow as I listen to Henri's voice—thick with his Dutch accent and muffled a bit on the scratchy recording—and I soak in his message, which is right on time for this Advent season.

In *A Spirituality of Waiting: Being Alert to God's Presence in Our Lives*, Henri focuses on the waiting people of Luke's Gospel—and, as it happens, of Advent and Christmas: Zechariah, Elizabeth, Mary, Simeon, Anna. "Waiting is never moving from nothing to something; it's always something to something. It's always from an already to more of it," Nouwen says. "If you really think about Zechariah and about Mary and about Elizabeth, you realize that they were living with a promise that nurtured them, that fed them, that made them able to stay where they are so that it could grow, so that it could develop."

A waiting person, in Henri's view, is someone who is "very present to the moment, who believes that this moment is THE moment."

Neither of those things—waiting or being present to the moment—is an easy proposition. Our world demands that we fill our days with more than we can handle. Doing, not being, is the mantra of our time. And waiting in any form seems like wasted time. In doctor's offices, in store lines, on hold with customer service—it's all a chore to most of us. Not to mention the pain that comes from the harder waiting—for the diagnosis, for a call from a loved one, for the job offer. As we stand on the cusp of Advent, can we see ourselves as waiting people, full of trust and promise rather than impatience or fear?

The Advent season invites us to put the world's ways aside and sink into the slow goodness of a spiritual season bedecked not in tinsel and bows but in silence and emptiness, in faint flickering lights against an inky winter sky and the Light that we know will break open our world and overcome its darkness forever come Christmas morning.

As you move through the pages of this book, remember that the waiting people of our faith story accompany us. They offer us inspiration and powerful reminders that so often it is in the waiting that we discover who we really are and who God has called us to be. Yes, the waiting is often the hardest part, but if we wait in hope, we will find that the waiting is also the most transforming part. Wait with me this Advent, and watch what God has in store.

FIRST WEEK OF ADVENT

Brave in Our Fear

Readings: Isa 2:1-5; Rom 13:11-14; Matt 24:37-44

Scripture:
Let us then throw off the works of darkness and put on the armor of light. (Rom 13:12b)

Reflection: Hanging outside the door to my office is an image of St. Joan of Arc in full armor, overlaid with a popular paraphrase of her rallying cry: "I am not afraid. I was born to do this." In reality, I am often afraid, and so I count on Joan's strength and determination to buoy me up when I'm flagging. We tend to think that Joan of Arc and others throughout the history of our faith were braver than the rest of us, willing to "put on the armor of light" and take on things we could not imagine. We may feel more in line with the great Southern Gothic writer Flannery O'Connor, who quipped in one of her short stories, "I think I could be a martyr if they killed me quick."

As we enter this Advent season, we are met not with the twinkling lights and the festive feel of the secular version of this season but with the hard truth and the ominous reminder of what it means to believe in a Savior who entered the world as a babe in a manger and died on a cross. We do not need the shiny armor of Joan as she charged into physical battle, but rather the armor of Christ, the sword and shield of a salvation won for us through his suffering. There is darkness all around—in the early nights outside our windows, in the headlines of sorrows at home and abroad, in the depths of our souls where we struggle to find our way. But today we are challenged to throw off that darkness and turn toward the Light that will be the only armor we need to do what we were born to do.

Meditation: Although we know intellectually that any day could be our last, we don't like to dwell on it. But meditating on our mortality is not morbid; it is often just the opposite. Today find a few minutes to dwell in this truth and let it inspire your thoughts, words, and actions.

Prayer: Lord of Eternal Life, as we move through the days and weeks of Advent, may we continually return to your promise of salvation amid the excitement and anticipation of this season. We want to live in and for you.

Willing, Not Perfect

Readings: Isa 4:2-6; Matt 8:5-11

Scripture:
The centurion said in reply, "Lord, I am not worthy to have you enter under my roof; only say the word and my servant will be healed." (Matt 8:8)

Reflection: The sight of a dark and threatening storm cloud in the distance can set us on edge if we're not close to shelter. We immediately go through a mental checklist: Was there a weather warning today? Is there danger of a tornado? Do I have my umbrella? Did I close the windows at home? Even when the gathering storm is totally out of our hands, we attempt to bring some control to the situation. It's as though we can offer ourselves and our loved ones protection through the power of our own worry.

   In today's readings, however, we are reminded that faith is not about figuring everything out on our own but about releasing the need to control, letting go and trusting that God is at the wheel, even if we're the ones driving down the highway. In the first reading from Isaiah, we breathe a sigh of relief as we hear that God's glory will be our shelter and protection no matter what comes at us. No checklist needed. But do we believe it? Then, in the Gospel—a healing story that we know so well and the words of the faith-filled centurion that we echo in every liturgy before Communion—we see the ultimate test of faith: believing in a miracle before it occurs, without seeing.

The centurion teaches not only about faith in God but about humility before God. We are, each one of us, unworthy to have Jesus enter under our roofs, into our lives, within our hearts. But there he is, always reminding us that we do not need to be perfect in our faith; we only need to be willing to trust.

Meditation: Ponder the centurion's words today. Say them out loud. Come back to them throughout your day. Do you truly believe that your soul can be healed and saved by God's word alone? Can you relinquish control and just trust?

Prayer: God our Protector, we know we can't navigate the storms of this life alone, no matter how hard we try. We pray you will be our shelter, our refuge, today and every day.

Jumping for Joy

Readings: Isa 11:1-10; Luke 10:21-24

Scripture:
"[F]or although you have hidden these things from the wise and the learned you have revealed them to the childlike." (Luke 10:21b)

Reflection: Usually when we hear the word "childlike," we don't see it as a positive thing. If someone were to call you "childlike," how would you feel? Probably not so great. But why is that? Jesus clearly understands that to be childlike is to be something wonderful. He turns the idea on its head.

Children are, after all, open and honest, joyful and kind. But over time we build a protective shield around ourselves. Those things seem too vulnerable, too weak, too soft. But it is precisely when we are willing to be open and vulnerable that we are most likely to hear the still, small voice of the Spirit, to recognize God in the everyday details of our lives.

When my son was three years old, we would take him out into the cul-de-sac near our house in Austin when the moon was high in the sky. He would stand there with his arms outstretched jumping and shouting, "I can't reach the moon!" Even at that tender age, he knew that actually reaching the moon was not possible, but his joy over seeing that big moon in the night sky filled him to overflowing and made him leap and shout.

Maybe this season of Advent is the time to dust off the soul-leaping joy we packed away when we became grown-up and "wise," time to shout out prayers to the heavens like a three-year-old trying to reach the moon. Ours is a faith built on a Savior who came to us as a baby—helpless, vulnerable, dependent. Now it's our turn. Can we come before the Lord like a child, arms outstretched, leaping for joy?

Meditation: Find something that makes you clap your hands with glee, something that sparks that childlike joy. Allow it to soften you just a bit. Feel contentment rising within, and then sit in silence and wait for God to whisper to your spirit.

Prayer: Gracious God, we hunger for a deeper relationship with you, but so often we refuse to let down our guard and let you into our hearts. Give us the courage to be childlike, the strength to be vulnerable.

Walking the Walk

Readings: Rom 10:9-18; Matt 4:18-22

Scripture:
"Come after me, and I will make you fishers of men." At once they left their nets and followed him. (Matt 4:19-20)

Reflection: Imagine for a moment that you are Andrew or his brother, Simon, minding your own business, casting your net, trying to earn a living. A scruffy-looking man, a complete stranger, asks you to follow him and become a "fisher of men," and you go without question, without looking back. Can you fathom it? I hate to say it, but I think I probably would have taken a hard pass on that offer. Too risky. Too unknown. Too radical.

Then again, the faith we profess today is all of those things and more: risky, unknown, radical, complicated, controversial, counter-cultural, and, let's not forget, beautiful and true. We may not have left our nets or walked away from our families, but we have, in a sense, abandoned ourselves to God—at least that's what we're called to do. Surely Andrew could not have known the trials and sufferings that lay ahead, or that he would die a martyr's death on a cross. And how often it is for us, that we say yes to something we believe God is calling us to, only to find that it involves more heartache and struggle than we initially bargained for.

Jesus promises eternal life, not an easy life. St. Andrew would remind us that not only is the Way not always easy, it's often quite difficult. Knowing that, do we run? No. We stand firm. And so in some ways we are very much like those apostles called to leave the safety of the familiar for the uncertainty of the unknown. Jesus, we trust in you.

Meditation: On this feast of St. Andrew, reflect on your life's work. How can your work become something that brings you closer to the heart of Jesus? Can you, like Andrew, follow where God leads without knowing where you will land?

Prayer: St. Andrew, intercede for us today, we pray, that we might gain the wisdom to know the path we should take, and the courage to walk it despite the trials that may come.

Shifting Sands

Readings: Isa 26:1-6; Matt 7:21, 24-27

Scripture:
"And everyone who listens to these words of mine but does not act on them will be like a fool who built his house on sand." (Matt 7:26)

Reflection: Today's readings speak of strong walls and ramparts, sturdy foundations and solid rock, and, conversely, collapsing sand and ruined houses—or, in the spiritual sense, ruined lives.

I certainly wouldn't be too keen on building a house on sand, having seen what it can do to even the tiniest sandcastle once the tide turns, no matter how pretty the turrets and seashell façade. And that's the heart of this problem. Are we worried about our façades and the surface decorations that make us appear to be strong and secure, or are we doing the deeper work that may not necessarily look pretty on the outside, but that sets our souls and our psyches into a mortar that won't shake even when those hurricane gale force winds come our way?

Jesus is the mortar, or, as he told us, the cornerstone (Matt 21:42). Without a life built up around and on Jesus, we are just one strong wave away from total collapse and ruin. Now is the time to shore up our construction. As we speed through

Advent toward Christmas, celebrating not just Christ's coming in the manger but his coming again at the end of time, we are keenly aware of how vital it is to get our spiritual houses in order.

Are we listening, really listening, to what Jesus has to say to us? Or are we paying him lip service and hoping no one will notice that we've built our houses on the shifting sands of a fickle world?

Meditation: Reread today's Scripture passages. Maybe even read them aloud. Find a phrase that speaks to you, and spend time in silence, contemplating that phrase. Come back to it throughout your day, listening to what Jesus is saying to your heart.

Prayer: Jesus, you are the cornerstone of all we are and all we do, the foundation upon which we want to build our todays, our tomorrows, and our eternity. You are our rock and refuge.

20/20 Spirituality

Readings: Isa 29:17-24; Matt 9:27-31

Scripture:
And out of gloom and darkness,
   the eyes of the blind shall see. (Isa 29:18b)

Reflection: Darkness and light, blindness and sight. The words of Isaiah and the words of Jesus pour over us, and we feel our own vision coming into sharper focus. "Do you believe that I can do this?" (Matt 9:28), Jesus asks the blind men in the Gospel of Matthew, and we hear it as if he is asking us that same question. Do we believe he can do what he says? Do we believe he really is who he says that he is? Do we see Jesus clearly, or is he clouded by the fog of worldly desires?

Even if we have 20/20 vision, we need Jesus to help us see who we are called to be and what we are called to do. If we look only through the lenses we've fashioned for ourselves, we will bump into walls and trip over the tree roots of best intentions and misguided perceptions. It is only when we, like the blind men, stand before Jesus and beg him to have pity on us and cure us that we can be made whole so we may see the world as it truly is and know where we need to go.

Think of Jesus as the progressive lens of spiritual midlife. Youth convinces us that we know where we're going. It is often only in midlife and maturity that we realize just how blurry our spiritual vision has become and turn back toward Jesus, recognizing that we do not know half of what we thought we knew. In fact, we may not even be sure we know what questions to ask in order to find the answers we crave.

Jesus is both the question and the answer. All we need to do is believe.

Meditation: Darkness can be frightening, suffocating, especially when we're in an unfamiliar place. A single light can transform the fear and give us hope. Jesus is that light, shining amid the darkness of our world, reminding us that we are never lost.

Prayer: Jesus, Light of the World, shine your truth into our hearts, chasing away the darkness that fills us with fear and prevents us from following where you lead. Yes, we believe!

December 3: Saint Francis Xavier, Priest

Practice and Preach

Readings: Isa 30:19-21, 23-26; Matt 9:35–10:1, 5a, 6-8

Scripture:
At the sight of the crowds, his heart was moved with pity for them because they were troubled and abandoned, like sheep without a shepherd. (Matt 9:36)

Reflection: In today's Gospel reading, Jesus feels great compassion for the crowds, who seem to him to be like sheep who are troubled and abandoned—or in the words of another translation, "harassed and helpless" (NRSV).

How many of us spend a good amount of our lives feeling harassed and helpless? We tend to trend toward self-pity, looking around at the filtered and curated Instagram lives of friends and acquaintances, and wondering why our clothes, our houses, our vacations, our children, and our dinner tables don't look like the picture-perfection we believe everyone else is relishing. Before you know it, a friend's award or accomplishment begins to feel like harassment, leaving us spiraling into a state of helplessness. We may wander through our lives unsure of how to find our way back to truth, back to ourselves. The only thing we're sure of is that we've been dealt a bad hand, and we deserve to wallow.

Today we see Jesus out among the crowds, gathering the lost sheep, those who are losing hope because they've been

18 *First Week of Advent*

harassed (probably in ways we can't imagine) and feeling helpless (probably because they suffered from real oppression and not just a bad day at the office). Jesus has compassion for them just as he does for us, even when we're not justified in our helpless feelings, and especially when we are. It doesn't matter where we fall on the spectrum, Jesus offers a way out, a way up. He gives us a different way, *the* Way. And if we are willing, we can throw off the mantel of self-pity and put on the garment of peace, the cloak of hope, the crown of salvation.

Meditation: Look at your life through the prism of today's Gospel. Are you among the throng feeling lost, or are you one being sent out to lift others up? "Preach the gospel at all times. When necessary, use words." That quote is famously attributed to St. Francis of Assisi, and although it's not likely he ever said those exact words, he lived their truth every day. What is your life preaching to others?

Prayer: We pray for the courage to put aside self-pity and preach through our very lives, to be guided by the gospel and draw others to Jesus through its powerful truth.

SECOND WEEK OF ADVENT

Welcoming the "Other"

Readings: Isa 11:1-10; Rom 15:4-9; Matt 3:1-12

Scripture:
Welcome one another, then, as Christ welcomed you, for the glory of God. (Rom 15:7)

Reflection: Today's readings offer a study in contrasts. Paul makes us feel uplifted and hopeful with his words of endurance and encouragement, harmony and welcome. John the Baptist, on the other hand, snaps us back to attention with his "brood of vipers" comment and warnings of the "unquenchable fire." There's no way to avoid feeling a little unsettled after the Gospel reading. Are we among the "brood"? Will we end up on the threshing floor? This is where these two seemingly disparate Scripture readings converge, offering us a choice. Will we be like the Pharisees and Sadducees who were warned by John, who thought they had reached a spiritual pinnacle but blocked others from entering the path to God (Matt 23:13)? Or will we model ourselves after Jesus, who welcomed not only existing believers but prostitutes and tax collectors, and so many others typically relegated to the margins?

Jesus came to save all, not just a few, and so we are called to welcome all, not just those who agree with our political or even our spiritual opinions. St. Benedict of Nursia wrote in his Rule that his monks should "receive all guests as Christ." It sounds so simple on the surface, but it's not always easy when "all" includes people who don't fit the mold we've created in our own minds.

Think of how dramatic it must have been when the disciples of Jesus began to welcome Gentiles and pagans into what had previously been a Jewish community. Who are the people we see as "other," and how can we soften our hearts and open our minds to welcome them to the table of the Lord as Jesus did, as Paul did, as we are called to do?

Meditation: Is there someone in your life who challenges you, someone you find difficult to welcome or love? Today, pray for that person and for your relationship, that Jesus will enter into the equation and bring peace where there was once discord.

Prayer: Jesus, Prince of Peace, open our hearts and minds to those who are different from us but who are our brothers and sisters all the same. May our human family be united in you, through you, and with you.

Risk vs. Reward

Readings: Isa 35:1-10; Luke 5:17-26

Scripture:
Say to those whose hearts are frightened:
    Be strong, fear not! (Isa 35:4a)

Reflection: Most of us live our lives surrounded by some element of fear. No matter how faithful we are, no matter how much we trust God, that fear factor seeps in now and then, sometimes more often than not. A nagging pain gets our minds reeling, a diagnosis sends us into the depths, a lost job, a broken relationship, an addiction, a dark night, a deep loneliness. Whatever it is that haunts us, fear comes along for the ride.

Over and over in Scripture, we are reminded to "be not afraid." Isaiah tells us again today that we shouldn't be frightened because God has come to save us, and, thankfully, our salvation doesn't depend on perfect health or a good job or a big social circle. We are saved simply because we are loved by God. We see that play out in the Gospel story today as well. The paralytic lowered down through the roof by his friends who took a crazy chance because they believed so strongly that Jesus could save. Their risk paid off: not only was their friend's condition cured, but his sins were forgiven as well. If they had let fear get in their way, get in their heads, they all would have been the worse for it.

It's not easy to set fear aside when our hearts are truly frightened. But if we come back to prayer, come back to breath, come back to silence, the fear starts to dissipate, and, even if we don't quite reach a level of outright courage, we can reach a place of trust, knowing that God will have our backs, and that with God we can get through anything.

Meditation: Sit in a comfortable chair and scan your body. From head to toe, release any tension. Bring your hands over your heart, and feel it beating; feel your inhales and exhales. Whenever fear rises, come back to this place and sit face to face with God.

Prayer: God of all faithfulness, we lay our fears before you today, knowing that only you can bring us peace, only you can heal our hearts, only you can save our souls.

Lost and Found

Readings: Isa 40:1-11; Matt 18:12-14

Scripture:
"In just the same way, it is not the will of your heavenly Father that one of these little ones be lost." (Matt 18:14)

Reflection: At some point in our lives, each of us probably falls into the category of the lost sheep that needs saving. Maybe we don't stop believing in God's plan, but we get off course and wander away on our own, following what appears to be a better plan, an easier path, or a more glamorous existence. Certainly, some are truly lost, not for a day or a week but for years, maybe even a lifetime. We may know them and love them and weep for them, wishing we could save them ourselves.

As painful as it is to experience or watch, being lost is not irreversible, as Jesus reminds us today. Jesus is always searching for us, waiting for us. Like a little sheep caught up on a rocky crag or down in a deep valley, we cry out as Isaiah urges to do in today's first reading. We question and plead, *Where are you, God?*, thinking it is God who is lost, and not the other way around. Our God may chase down the one that is lost, but he never abandons the ninety-nine who remain. We are forever bound, forever loved, forever called by the One whose voice we recognize no matter how far off course we get.

And it's easy to get off course. No life is without pain or tragedy, heartbreak or disillusionment; it is just the nature of being a broken human in a broken world. But our God is always just a prayer away. Closer, in fact. As soon as we turn to face God with our hearts and souls, the connection is made, even without words, and we are found.

Meditation: Put yourself in today's Gospel. Are you the one who is lost, or are you among the ninety-nine? How does it feel to be where you are? What is Jesus saying to you? Even if you are not lost, have you been found?

Prayer: Jesus, you are my North Star, my compass and my anchor. Speak my name, and I will recognize your voice and fly to your side, secure among your flock, found and free.

December 7:
Saint Ambrose, Bishop and Doctor of the Church

World Weary

Readings: Isa 40:25-31; Matt 11:28-30

Scripture:
"Take my yoke upon you and learn from me, for I am meek and humble of heart; and you will find rest for yourselves." (Matt 11:29)

Reflection: When we think of a yoke—perhaps an image of two oxen yoked together and plowing a field—we don't tend to think of it as a way for us to find rest. How can we find rest by putting *on* a yoke? Well, if we have not yet yoked ourselves to Jesus, it means we're carrying the load ourselves, pulling the plow of life behind us with no one to share the burden. In today's Gospel, Jesus invites us to let him walk alongside us and help us carry all the heavy things that weigh us down.

Jesus knows the burdens life puts on us. This is a gift of an incarnational God who chose to become one of us in order to save us. We are in the very midst of preparing for that great history-changing miracle, but we often forget the power behind the babe swaddled in a manger. Our God walked this earth and carried his own share of heavy burdens, including the actual physical burden of carrying the cross for his own crucifixion.

Our God does not want us to travel our own personal Calvary alone, falling under the weight of life's sorrows. He wants to lift us up, yoke himself to us forever, and be our rest and refreshment. We often yoke ourselves to things that do nothing to lift us up but instead tear us down—food, alcohol, overwork, social media, gossip, gambling. Jesus challenges us to throw off the old yoke and try on the yoke he offers us today. Are we strong enough to allow ourselves to be weak before God?

Meditation: What yoke have you been carrying for too long? Maybe it's a bad habit or toxic friendship. How would it feel to experience life without that familiar yoke? Pray today for the courage to lay down that yoke, and yoke yourself to Jesus instead.

Prayer: Merciful God, we are weary from the worldly burdens we carry, often of our own choosing. Give us the strength and willingness to lay down our own yokes and pick up yours.

December 8:
The Immaculate Conception of the Blessed Virgin Mary

A Graced Life

Readings: Gen 3:9-15, 20; Eph 1:3-6, 11-12; Luke 1:26-38

Scripture:
And coming to her, he said, "Hail, full of grace! The Lord is with you." (Luke 1:28)

Reflection: The words of the Hail Mary are so familiar, they tumble from our mouths like our own names, like the air we breathe. So infused are we with the words of this beloved prayer that at times it can be almost too familiar, too easy to let it roll off the tongue without spending time on each line, each word.

Bishop Edward B. Scharfenberger of Albany suggests that we pause when we get to the name of Jesus. The "pause" is an especially powerful prayer practice. Pausing at the name of Jesus reminds us that this prayer to our Blessed Mother is really all about Jesus, because Mary is always all about Jesus. Even today, when we celebrate Mary's Immaculate Conception, the Gospel is about *Jesus'* miraculous conception. It's no wonder people often confuse today's feast with that of the Annunciation.

Let's put the spotlight back on Mary for a moment and ponder those words spoken by the angel: "Hail, full of grace! The Lord is with you." Even before Mary's *fiat*, her yes to the angel's news, she was "full of grace." That's what made her ready to be the mother of the Messiah, the mother of God. She entered this world full of grace and lived her life full of grace. She accepted the angel's word, full of grace, and watched her Son die on a cross, full of grace. We can never know what was going through Mary's mind when the angel gave her the news, but we can guess what was going through her mind and heart: *Yes, Lord, always yes. Full of grace.*

Meditation: Pray the Hail Mary today. Slow this familiar prayer down, spending time with each line, turning the words over in your mind. When you reach the name of Jesus, pause and spend a moment in silence before you move on.

Prayer: Holy Mother Mary, on this beautiful feast of your Immaculate Conception, we ask you to intercede for us, that we might open ourselves up to God's grace as you did throughout your life.

People Pleasing

Readings: Isa 48:17-19; Matt 11:16-19

Scripture:
Jesus said to the crowds: "To what shall I compare this generation?" (Matt 11:16a)

Reflection: People can be hard to please. We are quick to judge, dismiss, gossip. Turns out it's an age-old issue. Jesus says as much in today's Gospel. He reminds people that they found fault with John the Baptist for one thing and fault with Jesus for just the opposite. Maybe people aren't necessarily looking for a savior but a mirror, and therein lies the problem. We cannot make God in our own image. Author Anne Lamott once wrote, quoting her good friend, Jesuit Father Tom Weston, "You can safely assume you've created God in your own image when it turns out that God hates all the same people you do."

John the Baptist challenged people to be sure, and he probably scared them a bit with his locust-and-honey diet and wild-man appearance. Those surface things gave people a good excuse to dismiss him as crazy or worse. And once his credibility was questioned, it gave people a good reason to ignore his difficult challenge to repent and change their lives. When Jesus enters the scene, you would think there would have been a sense of relief. Here was someone who seemed mild-mannered and kind, who spoke in stories rather than dire rants. But relief soon turned into its own kind of shaming and blaming as the people put Jesus' merciful and self-giving actions up to the mirror and asked themselves if this is what Jesus did, would they be expected to do the same? And so, the discrediting and whispers began.

From his birth, when Herod was set on destroying him, to the cross, when the crowds turned on him, Jesus—like John before him—made people uncomfortable because he threatened the status quo.

Messiah or mirror? It's our choice.

Meditation: "You pray best when the mirror of your soul is empty of every image except the Image of the Invisible Father," wrote Thomas Merton, giving us food for thought. Today when you pray, see what it feels like to begin to clear your interior mirror.

Prayer: God of justice, we know we are fickle followers. We clamor for your attention and then hide from your view. Today we pray for the ability to live up to your teaching, no matter how challenging.

The Kingdom Among Us

Readings: Sir 48:1-4, 9-11; Matt 17:9a, 10-13

Scripture:
"[B]ut I tell you that Elijah has already come, and they did not recognize him but did to him whatever they pleased." (Matt 17:12)

Reflection: Jesus gives his disciples then—and us now—a glimpse into just how much we might be missing as we move through life at breakneck speed, thinking we know the score. The people at the time are awaiting Elijah's return, and Jesus tells them, essentially, you're too late. He was already here. They eventually get that he's referring to John the Baptist—not because John the Baptist was some sort of resurrection or reincarnation of Elijah; he was not. But because he came, as Scripture prescribed, in advance of the Messiah, to prepare the way. "So John the Baptist has come in the spirit and power of Elijah," said Dominican Friar Matthew Jarvis in a homily delivered in Oxford, England, and published on the friars' blog. "This Advent we have the opportunity to hear this truth again, to accept it, and to share it—because the ramifications are extraordinary."

What are those ramifications for us today, right now? How does this ancient story affect our everyday lives? Father Jarvis offers an answer: "If John the Baptist has proclaimed the coming of the Kingdom and the forgiveness of sins, Jesus himself is telling us that the Kingdom is here and now among us."

Now is the perfect time to reflect on the message of John the Baptist and our own preparations for the coming of the Lord at Christmas and at the end of time.

Meditation: Contemplate these words from the Canticle of Zechariah: "In the tender compassion of our God / the dawn from on high shall break upon us, / to shine on those who dwell in darkness and the shadow of death, / and to guide our feet into the way of peace" (Luke 1:78-79).

Prayer: Jesus, like John the Baptist, may we know in our hearts the true way of humility: "He must increase; I must decrease" (John 3:30). May we let go of our pride and power so that you may increase in us.

THIRD WEEK OF ADVENT

More than a Prophet

Readings: Isa 35:1-6a, 10; Jas 5:7-10; Matt 11:2-11

Scripture:
[H]e sent his disciples to Jesus with this question, "Are you the one who is to come, or should we look for another?" (Matt 11:2b-3)

Reflection: We know enough of John the Baptist's life to know he didn't do anything halfway. He preached repentance and announced the coming of the Messiah, the one whose sandal he was not fit to unstrap, the one who would baptize with fire and the Holy Spirit (Mark 1:7-8).

With our 20/20 spiritual hindsight, we assume John had some insider tip that let him know Jesus was the One. But in today's Gospel, from his prison cell, he makes clear he doesn't know; in fact, he wonders if he should be looking for someone else. Let that reality sink in. Is there anything in your life for which you would give up everything and risk imprisonment and even death without absolute certainty about the one you were proclaiming? In a world where we like to know everything the minute it happens, preferably a minute before, it's hard to imagine the complete and utter trust in God that John's mission required.

"John the Baptist is the summit of the whole Jewish tradition. . . . He will be the great prophet who, with his own finger, can point to the Messiah, the Christ, and thereby the coming of the kingdom," writes Trappist Father Theophane Boyd in *Sundays at the Magic Monastery*. This is no mere holy man, and yet even this holiest of holy men has to act completely on faith. He knows the Light of the World is coming, even as he is left in the dark of uncertainty.

God doesn't ask even a fraction of this fortitude and faith from us, but how easily we back away and question God's plan. Trust. Faith. Prayer. Action. That was John's recipe. It should be ours as well.

Meditation: Do you ever feel as though God is nudging you to do something—or stop doing something? Do you shy away from taking action out of fear? What would it take to have John's total trust and leap into God's arms?

Prayer: God who is, and was, and is to come, we trust in your word. Give us the devotion and determination of John the Baptist as we strive to put our faith into action in service to others.

One of Us

Readings: Zech 2:14-17 or Rev 11:19a, 12:1-6a, 10ab; Luke 1:26-38 or Luke 1:39-47

Scripture:
"Blessed are you who believed that what was spoken to you by the Lord would be fulfilled." (Luke 1:45)

Reflection: Out in my backyard garden is a three-foot plastic statue of Our Lady of Guadalupe that has long had a special place in my life. Years ago, I had my heart set on just such a statue but didn't have much hope of finding one in upstate New York. Then one day, as I walked toward the garden section of the local Walmart, there she was, standing eye to eye with me from her shelf. I put her in my cart and proceeded to wheel the Blessed Mother around Walmart while I finished my shopping.

She took up residence in a raised flowerbed where I can see her from my kitchen, my family room, and my deck. She is our centerpiece, but now her brilliant colors have faded, there's a big crack down her back, and more often than not, she's tipped over into the oak tree. I hold onto her, though, not only for the constant reminder of Mary's role in my life but because this particular statue depicts Mary as the Aztec she was when she appeared in Tepeyac, dark-skinned and dark-haired. All the other statues of Our Lady of Guadalupe that I have seen are fairer-haired and paler-complexioned, which distorts the story and Mary's role as mother to us all.

Our Lady of Guadalupe was so powerful in bringing people to Jesus precisely because she appeared to the Mexican people as a Mexican. Mary was relevant to them because she was one of them. Like Elizabeth, we see Mary and know at once we are in the presence of someone special, someone touched by God but also very much like us. Mary is mother to us all.

Meditation: Reflect on your relationship with Mary. Do you have a special devotion to her under a particular title or role? Sit with Mary today and just let her be your mother. Let her comfort you as she once comforted her Son.

Prayer: Our Lady of Guadalupe, patroness of the Americas, we pray that there may be peace in our world, peace in our communities, and peace in our families. Blanket us with your motherly protection and love.

Just Feed One

Readings: Zeph 3:1-2, 9-13; Matt 21:28-32

Scripture:
"Which of the two did his father's will?" (Matt 21:31a)

Reflection: I'll take "Uncomfortable Gospels" for $500. That's how today's Gospel reading makes me feel. I squirm a bit, trying not to count how many times I've convinced myself I would do something, only to let it slip away out of fear or laziness or plain old disinterest. Of course, if I'm honest, I probably have quite a few marks on the plus side for the times I said I *wouldn't* do something but plowed ahead and made it happen in spite of myself! The bottom line: at one time or another, we've all been both of these sons.

So, what is the lesson Jesus is trying to get through to us today? I think the point is that those of us who show up for Mass every Sunday but don't live out the gospel in our day-to-day lives are less likely to be doing God's will than those who don't profess publicly but quietly go about doing the work of a believer without getting any of the "credit." The label "Christian" isn't a magic spell; we have to do the work to make it real.

We look to the role models who walked the walk—Francis of Assisi, Dorothy Day, Damien of Moloka'i. These were holy people who put others above all else, taking the gospel at face value and living it day by day. Most of us are not called to that kind of radical service, but we can still do the will of the Father without leaving all that we know. The opportunity to serve is all around us, not just in the inner cities or rural outposts, but across the dinner table and down the street.

Meditation: "If you can't feed a hundred people, then feed just one." This saying is often attributed to Mother Teresa. Even if she didn't say it, the sentiment hits home. It's easy to discount flying around the globe to feed the hungry in Calcutta; it's something else to discount driving across town to feed a hungry child. Where can you begin?

Prayer: Dear God, open my eyes to the needs right where I live so that I may do your work here on earth and put the gospel lessons into action. I want to do your will.

December 14: Saint John of the Cross,
Priest and Doctor of the Church

Land of Enchantment

Readings: Isa 45:6c-8, 18, 21c-25; Luke 7:18b-23

Scripture:
I am the LORD, there is no other. (Isa 45:6c)

Reflection: "The world is charged with the grandeur of God," Gerard Manley Hopkins wrote in his famous poem "God's Grandeur." And, based on what we hear in the first reading from Isaiah today, we are not to waste all the goodness and beauty that has been placed before us. It's as though God is urging us to stop and look around, to take it all in and remember, *God is God.* As if to say, *How do you think all of this got here?*

In her book, *Earth: Our Original Monastery,* Christine Valters Paintner dives into the idea of creation as the place where we can reconnect with the divine and suggests not only seeing goodness but experiencing "enchantment" right where we live. "Practicing enchantment is a commitment to seeing the world through new eyes. It means shaking off our cynicism and numbness and rediscovering the world that shimmers behind the everyday." That can be easy if we are in some beautiful locale—a beach, a mountain, a meadow full of sunflowers. Seeing the beauty in the everyday places and moments can be more of a challenge. But once we start to look, the spark of the divine is so obvious that we'll be shocked we missed it before.

Back in warmer days, I was kayaking on a quiet lake and came upon a massive rock at the lake's edge. Out of a crevice in the rock a tree was growing. A full tree. I went back to my room and wrote in my journal, "Nature finds a way." But the truth is that God finds a way. Because God is God, and there is no other. Isn't that enchanting?

Meditation: Trappist Brother Paul Quenon writes in his book *In Praise of the Useless Life* that he spends thirty minutes outside every day, no matter the weather. "One day may be Eden, another a dim limbo. Each mood molds my soul to its profile." Go outside and let the mood mold your soul.

Prayer: God of all creation, you are above and below and in every atom of our being. Thank you for a world that is at once breathtaking and heartbreaking. At every turn, we praise your name.

Mountain of Love

Readings: Isa 54:1-10; Luke 7:24-30

Scripture:
Though the mountains leave their place
  and the hills be shaken,
My love shall never leave you
  nor my covenant of peace be shaken,
  says the LORD, who has mercy on you. (Isa 54:10)

Reflection: From my window, I can see an unshakable mountain outside the hermitage where I am writing in the Adirondack Mountains of upstate New York. I try to imagine that mountain leaving its place, as Isaiah writes so poetically in today's first reading. It might be shaken, but disappear completely? I don't think so. And so is God's love, but even greater, even more unmovable, and, unlike a mountain, completely unshakable. After reading this passage, I found myself singing the words to an old St. Louis Jesuits song: "Though the mountains may fall and the hills turn to dust, yet the love of the Lord will stand."

I'm blessed to be surrounded by mountains where I live. Look in any direction and they're there, unmoving—Adirondack, Catskill, Berkshire, Green. They are at once imposing and inviting. That's how we often see our God: imposing and inviting. Isaiah tries to drive home the fact that God will never abandon us, and even if we should run, God will draw us back, again and again, no questions asked, like the father in the story of the Prodigal Son.

We are the ones who do the imposing most of the time, not God. We assume that because we have turned from God, we're not welcome back, and we impose exile upon ourselves. Or we soak in self-induced guilt, thinking we are unworthy and cannot possibly be loved, and we impose upon ourselves a sentence of despair. But God is our shelter in the storms we create. All we have to do is turn and face the unshakable mountain of God's love.

Meditation: Think about the times you've felt far from God. That feeling often comes from a decision we've made that breaks our relationship with God. Can we forgive ourselves? Can we go to the sacrament of reconciliation? Can we allow ourselves to return to our rightful place within God's loving embrace?

Prayer: We give thanks for your unconditional and unshakable love, O Lord. We release the self-imposed punishments we've allowed to chain us down, and we stand before you, exiles who have returned to our home, our shelter.

The Cross of Christmas

Readings: Isa 56:1-3a, 6-8; John 5:33-36

Scripture:
The works that the Father gave me to accomplish, these works that I perform testify on my behalf that the Father has sent me. (John 5:36b)

Reflection: As we move through Advent, pondering readings that often seem unrelated to the big celebration just around the bend, we are given a glimpse of Jesus' progression from a relative unknown to the Messiah he was born to be. In today's Gospel, Jesus continues to preach to the followers of John the Baptist, telling them in various ways that John was the messenger, the prophet foretold in Jewish Scripture, preparing the way for the One. Jesus never comes out and tells them who he is; he gives them background and metaphors, in hopes that the people will put two and two together.

All these centuries later, we need the same gentle-but-forceful scriptural brick over the head to remind us who it is we are preparing to celebrate. Not just a baby, not just a prophet, not just a holy man, but the Messiah, the Christ, the Savior of the world, and our own personal Savior. We know that throughout his years of ministry, Jesus performed many signs and miracles, and still he was hung on a cross. We know throughout our lives that Jesus has done the same for us in big and small ways, and still, we often don't want to think about the cross. It's more comforting to think of the baby lying in the manger.

Jesus did not come to comfort the world but to save it, and he told us in a multitude of ways that if we follow him, we, too, will be uncomfortable at times, maybe even to the point of true suffering. Christmas is coming, but it includes the cross. Do we still want to celebrate?

Meditation: Find a crucifix and put it among your Christmas decorations as a not-so-subtle reminder that we cannot have one without the other. Come back to the cross daily. Pray for the strength to face whatever cross you are carrying today.

Prayer: Jesus, our Savior, we prepare for your birth knowing it will lead to Calvary and the cross. We want to follow you with our whole hearts, minds, bodies, and spirits. Make us strong in your sight.

Family Tree

Readings: Gen 49:2, 8-10; Matt 1:1-17

Scripture:
. . . Jacob the father of Joseph, the husband of Mary. Of her was born Jesus who is called the Christ. (Matt 1:16)

Reflection: It's always powerful to hear the genealogy of Jesus proclaimed, not only because it traces Jesus' family line back to Abraham, but because of the names from Scripture that flow by—the majestic and the misfits, the adulterers and the murderers. This family had it all. Christian author Ann Voskamp sums it up, "Family gives you context and origin. It gives you understanding, and the family tree of Christ always gives you hope."

That's my takeaway from the opening lines of today's Gospel: hope. If some of those people can be included in the lineage of the Messiah, well then, I think you and I are more than fit to be among his followers! We usually don't remember that. We imagine Jesus' family was perfect, like he was. Immaculate, like Mary was. Protective and peaceful, like Joseph was. But you don't have to dig too far back to find the skeletons in the closet, and that's a beautiful thing. It means that no matter what our history, no matter who is in our past, no matter what sins they or we have committed, we have a place at the table and a promise of salvation.

Family is where we find the people who know us best, or think they know us best, and who can push our buttons in record-breaking time. Family is also our first community of faith, and a place where we are always welcome and always loved, warts and all. Sadly, for many, that's not always the reality. Jesus' family tree reminds us that we are never alone, and that we are part of a family that is not confined by bloodlines or borders.

Meditation: Pray for your own family today, those you live with and those you grew up with, those who went before you, and those who challenge you. Is there someone you need to forgive? Or maybe you need forgiveness? Give it all to the Lord.

Prayer: Jesus, we pray today for families. Give us the grace to love and forgive, to protect and accept. We pray in a special way for families that are struggling, and for those who do not feel welcome in their own families.

FOURTH WEEK OF ADVENT

Follow the Signs

Readings: Isa 7:10-14; Rom 1:1-7; Matt 1:18-24

Scripture:
The Lord spoke to Ahaz, saying: Ask for a sign from the Lord, your God; let it be as deep as the netherworld, or high as the sky! (Isa 7:10-11)

Reflection: Today's conversation between God and Ahaz made me laugh—in the best way—when I read it early one morning after sitting in prayer and telling God how fearful I was of too many things to list. And, as always, I prayed and wished for a sign, any sign, that might lead me on the right paths and give me a clue as to how to be who I am called to be. Then I walked downstairs to write this reflection, opened the lectionary to the day that was next on my calendar, and saw today's reading from Isaiah, reminding us that God wants us to ask him to guide us and to give us signs as outrageous as anything we can imagine.

But we, like Ahaz, often back away from that offer, maybe out of humility, but probably out of fear for what the sign we get might tell us or ask of us. And God, having had it *up to here* with Ahaz, like a frustrated father who says to his relentless children, "Don't make me come down there!" does just that. He decides to come down here. He doesn't just send a sign; he *becomes* the sign, by way of Mary, in the person of Jesus. A sign so outrageous it rocked the world, changed history, and continues to ripple outward in an endless pool of mercy and salvation and hope.

But have we let it change us?

Meditation: When was the last time you prayed for a sign? Sometimes all that's required to find what we are seeking is a sliver of silence so we can hear God. The signs are all around us. Can we stop our spinning long enough to notice?

Prayer: God of all goodness, we know you will lead us on right paths. Give us eyes to see the signs you have set before us. Give us courage to follow where you lead.

Faith and Hope

Readings: Judg 13:2-7, 24-25a; Luke 1:5-25

Scripture:
"So has the Lord done for me at a time when he has seen fit to take away my disgrace before others." (Luke 1:25)

Reflection: Although Zechariah and the angel Gabriel are the stars of today's Gospel, with the news of John the Baptist ringing on the angel's lips (if angels have lips!), and Zechariah struck silent in his disbelief, it is Elizabeth who steals the show in the final moments. Her words provide such honesty and comfort that we can see ourselves in her despite having nothing in common, except perhaps our own sense of despair.

Elizabeth waited her entire life for God to take away the "disgrace" she experienced in the eyes of others, and probably deep within her own heart and soul. How many of us live with disgrace—real or imagined or forced upon us by others—day after day, wishing for a different reality, a second chance, an opportunity to show the world that we are not who others say we are? And just when we think our time has passed and the window of opportunity seems to be closing fast, the Spirit of God sweeps through our figurative houses and rearranges not only the furniture but the doors and windows and the very ground we stand on!

Like Elizabeth, we may find ourselves transported in an instant to a place we never thought we'd be, realizing that we should have known God's time is not our time. Indeed, we can never be sure when or how our prayers will be answered, for the answer we get may not be the one we expected at all.

Meditation: So many of us live with shame or despair, forgetting that God in his mercy loves us through whatever it is that we think causes us "disgrace." God makes us whole, even when we see only empty spaces and flaws.

Prayer: Merciful Lord, may we recognize your love rushing in to fill the voids we create out of fear or shame. And may we, like Elizabeth, remain patient in faith and hope day after day.

The Grace of Yes

Readings: Isa 7:10-14; Luke 1:26-38

Scripture:
Then the angel said to her, "Do not be afraid, Mary, for you have found favor with God." (Luke 1:30)

Reflection: One thing becomes abundantly clear as we listen to the words from Luke today, a story so familiar to us that we might gloss over it as old news: *Finding favor with God does not mean life will be easy.* In fact, as was the case for Mary, it might mean just the opposite.

How often do we imagine that if we pray hard enough, give enough, do enough, be enough, we can spare ourselves and our loved ones the pain and heartache that beset most people at one time or another? Following the path of God, however, has never meant the road gets easier. Life is life, and it will come with hardships and illness, loss and sorrow, along with the joys. Our job, then, is not to pray our way to a perfect life but, like Mary, to accept with grace whatever comes our way and to trust that with God's help we can get through it.

But that's no small task. The Gospel makes it seem as though it was easy for Mary. We see a brief mention of her being "greatly troubled," and then move straight to her *fiat*, her yes. But as we know, Scripture doesn't always move along a straight line according to our modern-day schedule. Mary may have been "greatly troubled" for a long time, maybe for the rest of her life, but she did not let the trouble stop her from moving forward, from saying yes to God and to the life she was called to live.

Meditation: Sit with Mary's words today ("May it be done to me according to your word"). Let them resonate in your heart. Imagine yourself in Mary's shoes for a moment. Now return to whatever challenging situation you currently face and see if Mary's example can offer you the strength to say yes and take the next step.

Prayer: Blessed Mary, we seek your prayers today as we face the challenges that trouble us. Help us to accept what God is placing in our lives without fear, to say yes in faith.

Promises and Plans

Readings: Song 2:8-14 or Zeph 3:14-18a; Luke 1:39-45

Scripture:
"When Elizabeth heard Mary's greeting, the infant leaped in her womb . . ." (Luke 1:41)

Reflection: When it comes to trusting that God will follow through on his plans and promises, no one shows us how to do it better than Mary. Elizabeth recognizes this immediately and with some awe when Mary greets her with the child Jesus growing in her womb. Mary's faith is palpable, her chosenness apparent in her very being and in the fact that she's standing on Elizabeth's doorstep, having risked an arduous journey based on the word of an angel. Mary did not let her own troubles and fears stop her from acting in love, no matter the cost. She did what she needed to do and trusted that God would take care of everything else.

Julian of Norwich, the fourteenth-century English anchoress and mystic, echoes that theme in her best-known quote, "All shall be well, all shall be well, and all manner of things shall be well," words that can seem either cloyingly saccharine or simply out of touch. But, if we remember that Julian, living in isolation in a cell and surviving an illness that brought her close to death, is not issuing a feel-good affirmation but rather a statement of trust in God's love, we begin to see that she, too, is walking in Mary's footsteps, and so must we. Julian's quote continues: "[F]or there is a Force of Love moving through the universe that holds us fast and will never let us go."

Mary carried that Force within her; Elizabeth recognized it; Julian and other mystics experienced it. It is up to us to trust that this same Force is guiding us home, and that all God's promises will be fulfilled.

Meditation: Many quotes from the saints may at first seem a little too pie-in-the-sky, but, when put in context, reveal lives of suffering and strength. Ours is not a faith built on greeting-card sentiments but on hard-won truths. What words call to you today, asking you to look below the surface?

Prayer: Dear God, we trust that all will be well in your time, if not in ours. It's not always easy to trust, but we begin again each day, believing in your promises and plans.

Give and Take

Readings: 1 Sam 1:24-28; Luke 1:46-56

Scripture:
I prayed for this child, and the Lord granted my request. Now I, in turn, give him to the Lord; as long as he lives, he shall be dedicated to the Lord. (1 Sam 1:27-28a)

Reflection: Answered prayers. They often bring immediate gratitude, but we tend to let that shine wear off once we've accepted our good fortune and assimilate it into our reality as "normal," maybe even deserved.

Hannah in today's first reading shows us the opposite extreme, in some ways almost too extreme for us to appreciate. She prayed for a son and, upon receiving a son, gave him back to the Lord. She literally left him at the temple! As we hear this reading, our modern ears may hear something a little unhinged in that decision by Hannah, but she knew Samuel would be about the Lord's work, and so she was willing to give back to God the gift God gave to her.

Mary echoes the sentiments of Hannah in the beautiful and familiar words of the Magnificat in today's Gospel. "The almighty has done great things for me, and holy is his name." In Mary's case, the gift she received was unexpected and frightening, and yet it is gratitude and not fear we hear her speak. This is pure gratitude—gratitude for God's goodness, no matter what answers are received, no matter what comes next.

So often we approach God as we would a vending machine: we put a prayer in, and get a favor out. And if we're really lucky, maybe we'll get more than we asked for, more than we deserve. We thank God in the moment, maybe say another prayer, light a candle, tell others—but would we have the courage to give everything back to God, as Hannah and Mary did? Could we pray for something and then, upon receiving it, turn it completely over to God's care?

Meditation: We hear very little from Mary in Scripture, but today she gives us so much it's almost hard to take it all in. Spend time with the words of Mary's canticle in today's Gospel, meditating on each line and what it meant for her then and for us today.

Prayer: Blessed Mary, your words give us hope and remind us of God's great mercy. Walk with us as we face all that scares us. Help us to remember the good things the Almighty has done for us.

Signs and Wonder

Readings: Mal 3:1-4, 23-24; Luke 1:57-66

Scripture:
All who heard these things took them to heart, saying "What, then, will this child be?" For surely the hand of the Lord was with him. (Luke 1:66)

Reflection: Our readings from Scripture this week are filled with prophets and signs, people whose lives were marked by God before they took a breath, men and women who walked God's path with singularity of purpose no matter what was happening around them. All of this of course is leading us toward *the* Sign, the One who will soon come into the world to fulfill everything that came before and to transform everything that will come after.

The birth of John the Baptist in today's Gospel inches us closer to the birth of the Savior, giving us a glimpse of the shock and awe that surrounded John's birth and how much more Jesus' entry into the world is likely to rock the foundation of everything everyone thought they knew about God, about the world, about salvation.

Transformation never happens on our own terms, at least not when we've turned our transformation over to God. Transformation requires us to allow God to refine and purify us—as we hear in today's first reading—to allow God to lead us where we may not want to go but *must* go in order to blossom into who we are called to be. Mary and Joseph and Elizabeth and Zechariah were all living their lives according to their own plans and traditions when God stepped in and gave them a new course, a different destination that no one could predict or even clearly see on any map or chart.

This is what God does. God upends our lives and, if we are willing to let go of the controls, guides us to places we never imagined possible.

Meditation: Today's Gospel is filled with such faith and hope—from Elizabeth's unlikely pregnancy and newborn son, to the name they choose, to Zechariah's speech suddenly returning in a flood of blessings. How often are we ready to lose hope? Can we hold on in faith, trusting in God's time?

Prayer: God of all Faithfulness, we look to Elizabeth and Zechariah today as models of complete trust in your word. We pray to have a faith so bold that we never doubt where you lead.

December 24: Saturday of the Fourth Week of Advent
(Christmas Eve)

The Way of Peace

Readings: 2 Sam 7:1-5, 8b-12, 14a, 16; Luke 1:67-79

Scripture:
"In the tender compassion of our God
   the dawn from on high shall break upon us,
   to shine on those who dwell in darkness and the
      shadow of death,
   and to guide our feet into the way of peace."
   (Luke 1:78-79)

Reflection: As we listen to the words of Zechariah in today's Gospel, can we imagine what he was feeling when he spoke those words, and what so many people of that time—and still in our time—believed the Messiah would do for them in literal ways? Many people in Zechariah's time expected the Messiah to bring about political revolution and eventual peace and prosperity for Israel. We too may believe that giving our lives over to God will mean earthly success and unending happiness.

But that was not God's promise then and it is not God's promise now. Trusting in God does not mean we get wealth and success, power and prosperity, or a free pass on life's troubles. It means we have a God who will love us through the troubles, a God who will never turn his face from us. In his *Prayer of Abandonment*, Thomas Merton, the famed Trappist monk, wrote: "I believe the desire to please you does in fact please you. And I hope I have that desire in all I am doing. I hope I will never do anything apart from that desire. And I know if I do this you will lead me by the right road though I may know nothing about it. I will trust you always though I may seem to be lost and in the shadow of death. I will not fear, for you will never leave me to face my perils alone."

Like Zechariah, the tender compassion of our God will guide our feet toward peace if we are willing to abandon ourselves to God's mercy and love.

Meditation: If someone promised you a kingdom, would you imagine wealth and power or resurrection and salvation? Our human minds crave wealth and power, but day after day we profess belief in resurrection and salvation. Can we accept delayed gratification? Delayed glory?

Prayer: My Lord God, we pray for the courage to abandon ourselves to your grace, your promise. We long for the way of peace spoken of by Zechariah. Guide our feet ever closer to your kingdom.

SEASON OF CHRISTMAS

Words Matter

Readings:
Vigil: Isa 62:1-5; Acts 13:16-17, 22-25; Matt 1:1-25 *or* 1:18-25
Night: Isa 9:1-6; Titus 2:11-14; Luke 2:1-14
Dawn: Isa 62:11-12; Titus 3:4-7; Luke 2:15-20
Day: Isa 52:7-10; Heb 1:1-6; John 1:1-18 *or* 1:1-5, 9-14

Scripture:
In the beginning was the Word,
 and the Word as with God,
 and the Word was God. (John 1:1)

Reflection: Everything we have been waiting for, hoping for, longing for is given to us today. From this day forward everything changes. It can feel a bit overwhelming as we try to grasp it all and what it means for each of us—from the poetry of Isaiah and the long, beautiful genealogy of Jesus to the messages of angels and the shepherds in their amazement. It's no wonder we sing out, "Joy to the World!" Our hearts are so full it's all we can do to keep from jumping up and down like a toddler about to tear into a brightly wrapped present.

In the midst of the excitement, the Gospel of John cuts through all of the details to the mystical heart of the matter: Jesus is the Word of God, the Logos, one and the same with God since before time began. And John assures us that if we live in him and with him, we will never be left in darkness, no matter how dark the world may seem at times, even in the midst of celebration and twinkling lights. "They shall name him Emmanuel, which means, 'God is with us,'" Isaiah prophesied (see Matt 1:24).

Although the Incarnate God who entered the scene and was laid in a manger in Bethlehem is not physically among us as he was 2,000 years ago, he is with us just the same—indeed, even more so—because he lived and died and rose again so that we might have life and have it more fully.

Jesus lights the way, the Word of God always present, if we are willing to listen, as St. Benedict said, with "the ear of the heart."

Meditation: Imagine you are in a field on a clear night when a messenger appears and says, "Go, your Savior is waiting for you." What would you do? Today, despite the lack of visible angels among us, the message is the same: *Go! Your Savior is waiting!*

Prayer: Jesus, our Emmanuel, we thank you for entering our world in order to bring light and love into the darkness of human suffering. We hope in your word and rejoice in your promises.

Ultimate Trust

Readings: Acts 6:8-10; 7:54-59; Matt 10:17-22

Scripture:
"When they hand you over, do not worry about how you are to speak or what you are to say. You will be given at that moment what you are to say." (Matt 10:19)

Reflection: About a year ago, I was called to give testimony in a sworn deposition. I had never done anything like that before, and I was so afraid of what was to come. I wasn't afraid because I had done anything wrong, but because I wanted to be sure I would have the answers to any questions and would be able to speak the full truth without doubting my memory or feeling unsure. Before I entered into the situation, I prayed to the Holy Spirit to give me the words I needed. I do the same just before I lead a retreat, give a talk, go on the radio, or begin an important work meeting. God promises us that if we trust, we will be given what we need when we need it.

Few of us will ever be called to have the kind of trust we see in Stephen in today's first reading, when he willingly gives up his life for the Truth. Unfortunately, there have been enough times in recent years that we have had reason to see such courage among Christians in other countries, and often, like Stephen, the name of Jesus is among the last words on their lips. Such profound faith, such unwavering trust.

God calls us to trust in things big and small, but often we are too afraid to let go and give ourselves over to the One who will always save us. Can we utter the name of Jesus with reverence when we are afraid and know that the Spirit will carry us where we need to go?

Meditation: Each time you encounter something today that causes you to worry, pause and call on the name of Jesus. Say the simple but powerful prayer of St. Faustina: "Jesus, I trust in you," and watch how those words change the landscape.

Prayer: Spirit of God, be with us in good times and bad. Give us the words we need, the courage we crave, the trust that will lead us home.

Poetry of Prayer

Readings: 1 John 1:1-4; John 20:1a, 2-8

Scripture:
We are writing this so that our joy may be complete.
(1 John 1:4)

Reflection: The poetry that is evident in the writings attributed to St. John, whose feast we celebrate today, capture not just a story but a feeling. From the opening words of the Gospel to the readings we hear today, we can read and feel and sense that John was truly filled with joy over the words and mission of Jesus Christ.

Today John writes that he is putting down these words "so that our joy may be complete." The joy was not just in the living and witnessing but in the sharing. The followers of Jesus, the ones who lived alongside him and saw him perform miracles, preach parables, die and rise again, were not content to keep the word to themselves or to know that as long as their lives were touched, their souls saved, that nothing else was required. No. In order to make the joy complete, to do what the Master asked of them, they had to share—write, preach, witness, maybe even die.

We are called to do no less. It is not enough for us to have a private relationship with Jesus, which is of course critical to our own faith journeys. We must share the Good News of

Jesus Christ, not necessarily through Bible-thumping or door-knocking, but by the way we live our lives, the truth we speak, the good we do, the way we love our neighbors.

Sometimes that's not a comforting thought when I look at my day-to-day actions compared to my profession of faith. And that's okay. We are human, and we can begin again every day.

Meditation: If someone were to look at the way you live your life, what would be their takeaway? A Dominican Friar at a Mass I attended preached that he doesn't believe there are atheists because everyone has something in his or her life that gets turned into a god, something that is valued above all else. What do you value? What are you sharing with the world?

Prayer: St. John, beloved disciple of Christ, help us to know the complete joy of living and spreading the gospel, as you continue to do through the poetry and power of your faithful witness written into the history of our lives.

Peaks and Valleys

Readings: 1 John 1:5–2:2; Matt 2:13-18

Scripture:
Beloved: This is the message that we have heard from Jesus Christ and proclaim to you: God is light, and in him there is no darkness at all. (1 John 1:5)

Reflection: We are just fresh off the glory and beauty of Bethlehem, and here we are today, plunged into darkness, weeping with Rachel for her children. How can this be? Don't we get to bask in the light for at least a little while?

Sadly, this is not just an account from a long-ago time in history; this is human life, daily life. We are not promised only mountaintop miracles and joy. The valleys are real and deep and often very dark. But John reminds us in today's first reading that there is no darkness in our God. If we keep our eyes and hearts and minds set on God, there will be a light, even if at times it feels like only a sliver. If we remain focused on the Light, the darkness will never overcome us.

I think back to when my children were small, and how they needed a tiny nightlight in the corner of their rooms in order to fall asleep. The tiny glimmer didn't mean they could see what was happening around them, but somehow that dim light shining in the darkness was enough to let them relax and trust. God is like that for each of us, a light shining in the dark corners of our souls, the places where worries fester and shames haunt.

But God will not leave us there. God keeps shining the light of his love into our lives, hoping that we will turn our faces toward him and feel the glow and let go of all that is making us weep so that God may carry the burden with us, for us.

Meditation: The Canadian songwriter Leonard Cohen wrote these striking words in *Anthem*: "There is a crack, a crack in everything. That's how the light gets in." Today look at the cracks in your life and notice where God's light is trying to shine through.

Prayer: God of Light and Love, we turn to you, like Rachel weeping for her children, and long for comfort and peace. Help us to hold onto your promise when we are in the deepest valleys of our lives.

December 29: Fifth Day within the Octave of the Nativity of the Lord

Multiple Choice

Readings: 1 John 2:3-11; Luke 2:22-35

Scripture:
This is the way we may know that we are in union with him: whoever claims to abide in him ought to walk just as he walked. (1 John 2:5b-6)

Reflection: Hate can be a sneaky thing. It can work its way into the crevices of our hearts and take up residence, quietly and without much fanfare, and therein lies the problem. While we might never say the words "I hate you" to someone (at least not to their face), we may harbor those feelings toward them in a powerful way, sometimes unwittingly.

Think of people who have wronged you terribly—I don't mean the small-but-hurtful things; I'm talking about the scarring, life-altering hurt. Maybe the hurt wasn't even against you personally but against someone you love, or maybe even some*thing* you love. I can't help but think of our church and the battle scars she bears from being mired in the scandal of priests who sexually abused children and bishops who were willing to look away. For many of us—including those who may have left the fold because of the scandal—these crimes and deepest of sins bring up a feeling toward the perpetrators that can only be described as hate.

The idea of loving those people as "brothers," as John instructs, is challenging if not repulsive.

Jesus' way is never easy, is it? Learning to love our enemies and to be kind to those who hurt us is not the human way, it is not the world's way, and, try as we might, it can be a very tall order even as we are committed to God's way. "Whoever says he is in the light, yet hates his brother, is still in the darkness" (1 John 2:9).

God offers us a choice—not an easy choice if we take the instruction to heart, but a choice all the same—darkness or light?

Meditation: Travel into the farthest reaches of your heart and seek out the hidden hate that might live there. When we do this, we can almost feel a physical reaction, a tension. Can we soften a bit and give God room to enter the space?

Prayer: God of mercy, soften our hearts toward those who have hurt us so that we may walk as Jesus walked and remain in the light of your love for all time.

Releasing the Reins

Readings: Sir 3:2-6, 12-14 or Col 3:12-21 or 3:12-17; Matt 2:13-15, 19-23

Scripture:
And let the peace of Christ control your hearts, the peace into which you were also called in one body. And be thankful. (Col 3:15)

Reflection: What would it be like if we could or *would* let the peace of Christ control our hearts, as St. Paul admonishes us today? Just imagining that possibility makes my shoulders relax and my jaw slacken a bit. It sounds so soothing, so refreshing, so impossible—at least for a type A personality like me! We usually feel like we need to be in control of everything, not only our own emotions and thoughts, but everybody else's as well. We fool ourselves into thinking that trying to control things will ease our worry and give us a sense of action and purpose. But usually it does just the opposite because, let's face it, we're never really in control.

Today, on this feast of the Holy Family, we can see the ultimate example of losing control or, more accurately, giving up control for something greater. How much did Mary, Joseph, and Jesus have to go through that was not according to their own plans? *None* of it was according to plan! Not the birth, not the fleeing, not the prophecy of a pierced heart.

And yet each one stepped away from the chaos and fear to say, "Yes." They went where the Lord was leading, even when it was a manger, a strange land, a road to Calvary.

Our lives are filled with fears, even when we live comfortably and peacefully relative to most. It is the nature of this thing called life. But Jesus holds out a promise of peace and invites us, *calls* us, to join him there, to give over whatever is haunting us, holding us down, keeping us fearful. Jesus calls us to give up control and gain our freedom at last.

Meditation: What is it that's keeping you fearful today? Where are you attempting to exert control and are losing the battle? Can you relinquish your hold on the reins just a bit? Can you hand the reins over to Jesus and rest in his peace?

Prayer: Jesus, Prince of Peace, we long for the faith of your Holy Family, faith that trusts without question, acts without fear. We ask for a sliver of this grace and peace in our own lives today. We give you the reins.

December 31: Seventh Day within the Octave of the Nativity of the Lord

Grace and Truth

Readings: 1 John 2:18-21; John 1:1-18

Scripture:
From his fullness we have all received, grace in place of grace, because while the law was given through Moses, grace and truth came through Jesus Christ. (John 1:16-17)

Reflection: Grace can be hard to put your finger on, like trying to catch a cloud or hold onto a breeze. Years ago while writing an introductory book about Catholicism, I struggled to define grace in a way that would make sense to people, especially people who had never really contemplated that word before. How do you describe something so ethereal and transcendent? We kind of get what it means on a gut-level, but putting it into words is another story. Bono, of the Irish rock group U2, sings in the song *Grace*: "Grace makes beauty out of ugly things. Grace finds beauty in everything." Because of grace, he sings, the things that used to hurt no longer do. It seems so simple when we hear it put it like that, doesn't it?

We all need grace to get through this life, to get through this day, but we have to want it and seek it and watch for it, or we're very likely to miss it when it's right there in our midst. In today's Gospel, John reminds us that those who follow Jesus will receive his grace, not just once, not just a little, but "grace upon grace" (NRSV). It's a gift we get for no other reason than simply showing up in this life and turning toward God.

The catechism defines grace as "the free and undeserved help that God gives us." The next time you can't quite put your finger on grace, just open yourself up to what is already there, and let God turn everything in your life to beauty.

Meditation: Look at your life right now, no matter where you are at this moment, and see if you can spot the grace that's available to you in the moment. If you can't, ask God to open your eyes to all that is yours.

Prayer: God of truth and grace, touch the dark corners of our lives and the ugly parts of our pasts with the light and beauty that Jesus came into the world to bring to each one of us.

January 1: Solemnity of Mary, the Holy Mother of God

Heart Work

Readings: Num 6:22-27; Gal 4:4-7; Luke 2:16-21

Scripture:
And Mary kept all these things, reflecting on them in her heart. (Luke 2:19)

Reflection: We all have moments in our lives—memories, both good and bad—that are stored away in our hearts. Now and then, on certain dates or when we hear a certain song or pick up a certain scent, we may find them rising to the surface of their own accord. With every beat of our hearts, these memories and moments feel as real as they did on the day they first occurred.

On this feast day, the Solemnity of Mary, the Holy Mother of God, we imagine a heart so full of memories and miracles, sufferings and sorrows, that we can almost feel the weight of them in our own hearts, the ache of keeping all those things inside with such grace and faith and trust. We don't ever see any scenes in Scripture where Mary loses it—as we might in our own lives at times—saying that she hates her life or crying out in anger, "Why me?" Instead, we see grace under pressure, a heart that is pierced but continues to beat fiercely, for God, for her Son, and for all of us.

This is an intimate bond we share with Jesus, a mother given to him by his Father and given to us by Jesus on the cross. His mother is our mother; God's mother is our mother.

What a tremendous gift, what an incredible truth, something to keep stored deep within our own hearts. When life is getting the best of us, we can allow it to rise to the surface and support us, reminding us that we are not alone, that we have a Savior and a mother who have felt it all.

Meditation: What does the word "mother" conjure up for you? For some it can be unconditional love. For others it could be a memory tinged with pain. Now turn your eyes toward our universal mother, Mary. Allow Mary to comfort you today. Speak to her, from your pierced heart to hers.

Prayer: Holy Mary, Mother of God, pray for us, your children, and lead us ever closer to your Son—the baby you bore, the child you raised, the man you beheld on the cross and in your arms.

Fast Forward

Readings: 1 John 2:22-28; John 1:19-28

Scripture:
He said:
"I am *the voice of one crying out in the desert,*
'Make straight the way of the Lord.'" (John 1:23)

Reflection: As we work our way toward the end of the Christmas season, we suddenly get a Gospel reading that makes us pause for a moment and wonder if maybe we haven't accidentally taken a leap into Lent by mistake. We go from the presentation and circumcision of the child Jesus to today's scene of John the Baptist prophesying about the One who is coming. It can feel a little disjointed at first. We want more of Mary, Jesus, and Joseph, more insights into their family, their home, their life. We want more details about what it was like to raise the boy who would be Savior of the world.

But Scripture does not provide us with those stories. We can imagine that Jesus learned how to be a carpenter alongside Joseph, that he learned how to grow in faith and love alongside his mother, that he learned Jewish traditions and prayers within his community, but we are not privy to those actual scenes or facts. What John tells us today is really all we need, however. Because the man who is the Messiah could not have reached that spiritual pinnacle without the guiding hands of Mary and Joseph throughout his childhood and young adult life.

We often talk about the "domestic church," the place at home among our families where we first learn about God and about how to love unconditionally. And so it would have been for Jesus, who will emerge on the scriptural scene to fill the world—and to fill each one of us—not only with the love and mercy of his heavenly Father, but with the love and compassion of his earthly parents.

Meditation: Put yourself into a missing scene from Jesus' youth. Are you playing outside his house with him? Learning the Torah with him? Waiting for him to deliver a newly built table? Imagine the young Jesus, learning and growing. Get to know the very human Jesus of Nazareth.

Prayer: Incarnate God, we thank you for becoming one of us, for knowing the pain and joy of being human, for walking on this earth as we do now, for entering this world in order to save it and us.

Children of God

Readings: 1 John 2:29–3:6; John 1:29-34

Scripture:
See what love the Father has bestowed on us that we may be called the children of God. Yet so we are. The reason the world does know us is that it did not know him. (1 John 3:1)

Reflection: John's words in today's first reading can be a lesson in frustration. He says we are children of God, and yet he also says, "No one who remains in him sins; no one who sins has seen him or known him" (1 John 3:6). I, for one, try and try again to "remain in him," but let me tell you, I sin and sin again. And I can't make that stop. Because I'm human.

We are all human. We cannot be what Jesus was because we are not God, and we cannot make ourselves into gods. I understand that John is poetic (and I love him for it), but for those of us in the cheap seats, this reading can be defeating. If we cannot belong to God despite our sin, how can we get up in the morning? How can we crawl on our spiritual knees to the feet of the Lord—and of those we've hurt—and beg for forgiveness and for a new beginning?

Our God is a God of second chances, of starting over, of never, ever saying, "You are too far gone to save." Of course, we have to read John's letter according to the time and place it was written, probably sometime around the end of the first century. Jesus was not a distant memory but a fairly recent reality. Now, more than two thousand years later, we know how deeply humans can sin, even when they profess belief in Jesus. We may not have known Jesus in the flesh, but we know him in our hearts, and we know that he sees and knows and loves us no matter what. Despair is not an option.

Meditation: We can be hard on ourselves when it comes to faith. We want to be perfect, and that's a beautiful ideal, but it's not reality. That's okay. We can begin again every day. Our mistakes do not define us because we are children of God.

Prayer: Heavenly Father, we want to avoid sin, but we struggle—against our ego, our desire to be liked, to be important, to be successful. Help us to stop striving and to rest in your love and mercy.

Lost and Found

Readings: 1 John 3:7-10; John 1:35-42

Scripture:
He first found his own brother Simon and told him, "We have found the Messiah," which is translated Christ. (John 1:41)

Reflection: Today we see the beginnings of discipleship. "Come and see," Jesus says, and those who hear him do— and they don't leave because what they see and hear keeps them rooted to the ground beside him. Andrew tells his brother Simon, "We have found the Messiah."

As modern readers, we take that all in stride. Ah, yes, they found the Messiah. But wait. What? *They found the Messiah!* This was not a casual thing; this was a life-shaking, world-flipping thing. Even Simon's named was changed. *Everything* changed in those moments when the apostles were called by name by the Messiah to follow him. The same is required of us. We can't simply say "Yes, yes, Lord" and carry on with life unchanged. If Jesus does not change us, then we are not listening to his words, because his words are revolutionary— not just in a global sense but in a personal sense. Dorothy Day, who lived the gospel of Jesus Christ as one called by the Master himself, said: "The greatest challenge of the day is: how to bring about a revolution of the heart. A revolution which must start with each one of us."

For Andrew and Simon in the Gospel today, meeting Jesus sparked that individual revolution and eventually a historical and spiritual revolution that changed our world for all time. We do not have to leave behind our nets or our families or even our comfortable houses, but we are called to leave behind our comfortable ideas and to go into the sometimes scary places Jesus calls us, trusting that everything is going according to plan, because we have found the Messiah.

Meditation: St. Elizabeth Ann Seton, whose feast we celebrate today, said: "O my God, forgive what I have been, correct what I am, and direct what I will be." This is how a revolution of the heart begins, with surrender.

Prayer: Jesus, you have called us by name. Give us the willingness to be made new by you and in you, to take the revolutionary step of total surrender to your will and your love.

January 5: John Neumann, Bishop

Love over Hate

Readings: 1 John 3:11-21; John 1:43-51

Scripture:
Everyone who hates his brother is a murderer, and you know that no murderer has eternal life remaining in him. (1 John 3:15)

Reflection: In the spirit of full disclosure, the morning I was preparing to write today's reflection was a bad day, coming at the end of a couple of bad weeks. As I walked to my computer, I thought of Thomas Merton's famous "Walnut and Fourth moment" when he stood on a street corner, looked around, and felt tremendous love for everyone standing near him, wishing he could tell them they were all "walking around shining like the sun." And I said out loud to myself (and I'm not proud of this), "Yeah, well, I hate everyone." (Don't judge me yet; the story gets better!) In my sorry state, I sat down at my laptop and looked up the Scripture citations for today's reflection. I opened 1 John 3, and my jaw dropped when I saw the line: "Everyone who hates his brother is a murderer." I said out loud again, "Well-played, God!"

Scripture never ceases to hold me accountable for whatever I might be thinking or feeling at the time I pick up the day's readings. But this one was rough. Am I really equal to a murderer? Are any of us who feel hate at any given moment? No, we are not literally murderers, but we are allowing very real evil into our hearts when we choose hate over love. So let's keep this tough verse close to us when the world is closing in and life is getting the better of us. It's a slippery slope from hate with our morning coffee to hate that hurts others directly.

Meditation: In the Marriage Encounter movement, there is a saying: "Make a decision to love." It's a daily choice, a minute-by-minute choice. This is not unlike the Alcoholics Anonymous motto: "One day at a time." Maybe we need to put the two together: Make a decision to love one day at a time.

Prayer: God of mercy, teach us to love as you do and to return to that love whenever we feel the first signs of hatred taking root in our hearts. We choose you one day at a time; we choose Love.

Tracing Our Roots

Readings: 1 John 5:5-13; Mark 1:7-11 or Luke 3:23, 31-34, 36, 38

Scripture:
. . . the son of Enos, the son of Seth, the son of Adam, the son of God. (Luke 3:38)

Reflection: We began the Christmas season with Matthew's genealogy of Jesus rooted in Abraham. Now, in the final days of the season, we come full circle to Luke's genealogy which goes a step further, linking Jesus' lineage all the way back to Adam and finally, to God. We often hear Jesus described as the new Adam (and Mary as the new Eve), making right what our first figurative parents got so terribly wrong, straightening the crooked lines written by those who make up the earliest link in our own spiritual lineage. Jesus is the "yes" to Adam's "no," the suffering servant who transforms the willful disobedience that closed us off from God for so long.

In the First Letter to the Corinthians, St. Paul writes: "So, too, it is written, 'The first man, Adam, became a living being,' the last Adam a life-giving spirit" (15:45). And in his letter to the Romans: "But death reigned from Adam to Moses, even over those who did not sin after the pattern of the tres-pass of Adam. . . . For just as through the disobedience of one person the many were made sinners, so through the obedience of one the many will be made righteous" (5:14, 19).

Our spiritual family tree reminds us that we are not bound to the mistakes of our past or to the story the world may want to write for us, because we have a Savior who broke us free of our bonds and, despite our own disobedience, won for us eternal salvation.

Meditation: What is your personal spiritual lineage? If you were to trace your faith back to its roots, what would emerge as pivotal? Recall the key figures and transformational moments. Who in your life today continues to guide you on that journey?

Prayer: Jesus our Brother, thank you for being the roots of our spiritual family tree, for providing the nourishment and strength we need. Help us grow in the light of your love.

Mother and Son

Readings: 1 John 5:14-21; John 2:1-11

Scripture:
And Jesus said to her, "Woman, how does your concern affect me? My hour has not yet come." His mother said to the servers, "Do whatever he tells you." (John 2:4-5)

Reflection: The exchange between Jesus and his mother in today's Gospel is at once familiar, enlightening, and even funny. A mother is a mother, after all, even when that mother is the mother of God! And Jesus, like any son or daughter might do, bristles at his mother telling him to do something that he does not believe he is ready to do. Mary, knowing full well she is talking not just to her son but to the Messiah, seemingly ignores him and tells the servants to do "whatever he tells you." As we know from this first miracle story in John's Gospel, Jesus does, in fact, do as his mother asked—a miracle at a party, a miracle that captures our hearts and our imaginations with its simplicity and joy.

Underpinning it all, of course, is Mary's bond with her son, a bond that tethers them not only to each other but to each one of us. We say the words of the Hail Mary confidently, knowing that, as she did for the wedding hosts at Cana, Mary will go to Jesus and plead on our behalf. For our part, we should then expect to do *whatever he tells us*. And that's not so easy. We often want the miracle without the required transformation. We want the prayer answered without having to do any spiritual work. We come to the feet of the Lord, to the heart of Mary, longing for something to soothe our parched souls, but we cannot receive God's flood of mercy unless we open our hands and our hearts to receive what God offers, no questions asked.

Meditation: Put yourself at the wedding feast today. Are you the worried host, the joyful bride, an oblivious guest, a servant bringing a jar of water and wondering what might possibly happen? Immerse yourself in this favorite story and see what unfolds.

Prayer: Blessed Mother Mary, we turn to you again and again in prayer, knowing you will intercede for us. *To Jesus through Mary.* May those words serve as our roadmap, our mantra, our hope.

EPIPHANY AND
BAPTISM OF THE LORD

Signs of Wonder

Readings: Isa 60:1-6; Eph 3:2-3a, 5-6; Matt 2:1-12

Scripture:
"Where is the newborn king of the Jews? We saw his star at its rising and have come to do him homage." (Matt 2:2)

Reflection: To "have an epiphany" means to suddenly perceive or understand something important, maybe even life-changing, and it usually occurs in seemingly ordinary moments and circumstances. We've all had those *Aha!* moments that wake us up out of our often unconscious stumbling through life, that instant when we see or hear or experience something that opens our eyes all at once to a reality we could not perceive just a few moments before.

It's no surprise that this term—"to have an epiphany"—grew out of one of the greatest *Aha!* moments of all time: the visit of the magi to the scene of the nativity in Bethlehem after a long and arduous journey. Theirs was a multi-part epiphany it seems, sparked first by a pinpoint of light in the sky and sealed by the scene of a babe in a manger. What we tend to forget is that even the *Aha!* moments that seem to come out of nowhere are usually built upon many small-but-significant moments that go unnoticed until the big reveal.

"A journey always involves a transformation, a change," said Pope Francis on the feast of the Epiphany in 2021. "After a journey, we are no longer the same. There is always something new about those who have made a journey: they have learned new things, encountered new people and situations, and found inner strength amid the hardships and risks they met along the way. No one worships the Lord without first experiencing the interior growth that comes from embarking on a journey."

May all of our journeys lead to epiphanies, and may our epiphanies transform us so we will never be the same.

Meditation: We are so used to having a GPS to guide every step of our way that we may not know how to be open to the unexpected anymore. When was the last time you let God set your course, even if it meant taking the more challenging route?

Prayer: God of wonder, we move through life so fast that we often miss the signs of your presence among us. Give us the patience to pause, to look up, to be awed and open and willing to walk wherever you lead.

Standing in Line

Readings: Isa 42:1-4, 6-7; Acts 10:34-38; Matt 3:13-17

Scripture:
After Jesus was baptized, he came up from the water and behold, the heavens were opened for him, and he saw the Spirit of God descending like a dove and coming upon him. (Matt 3:16)

Reflection: As we enter the scene at the Jordan River in today's Gospel, we may find ourselves asking the very same question John the Baptist asks: Why is Jesus coming to be baptized by John and not the other way around? Although it's a powerful moment, it can be a confusing moment as well. I've heard preachers do all kinds of homiletic acrobatics with this one, but I think it comes down to something much simpler and clearer than we might expect.

Jesus, who was without sin, came to take on the sins of the world. He was not baptized because he needed his sins forgiven (he didn't have any) but because we need *our* sins forgiven—just as he would later suffer and die on a cross for us through no fault of his own. This is how much our God loves us. Our God breaks into this crazy human world, with all its heartache and pain, and experiences it like we do in order to save us from ourselves.

Jesuit Father James Martin shared this perspective-shifting insight about Jesus' baptism: "One possible explanation of why Jesus chose to be baptized is that he meant it as a sign that he was on board with John's larger mission. He wanted to take his place with the rest of the Jewish people who were following John at the time. In that way, it's really a radical act of humility on Jesus' part. Imagine him standing in line waiting to be baptized with everyone else. And it's another indication of how much God wanted to be with us. At the baptism God stood in line."

Meditation: In Matthew's account of Jesus' baptism, "he [Jesus] saw the Spirit of God descending like a dove," but it is unclear whether anyone else saw this happening. To others, Jesus may have simply appeared to be another Jewish man waiting his turn. How often is God right beside us in everyday life and we don't realize it?

Prayer: Incarnate God, thank you for becoming one of us in order to save us. May we recognize your presence in the faces of our brothers and sisters, and in the ordinary moments of our lives.

References

Introduction
Henri J.M. Nouwen, "A Spirituality of Waiting: Being Alert to God's Presence in Our Lives" (Notre Dame, IN: Ave Maria Press, 2014).

November 27: First Sunday of Advent
Flannery O'Connor, "A Temple of the Holy Ghost," in *A Good Man Is Hard to Find and Other Stories* (Orlando: Harcourt, 1955), 95.

December 4: Second Sunday of Advent
St. Benedict of Nursia, *The Rule of St. Benedict* (New York: Image Books, 1975), 43.

December 9: Friday of the Second Week of Advent
Anne Lamott, *Bird by Bird: Some Instructions on Writing and Life* (New York: Doubleday, 1994), 22.
Thomas Merton, *Thoughts in Solitude* (New York: Farrar, Straus and Giroux, 1956), 113.

December 10: Saturday of the Second Week of Advent
Matthew Jarvis, OP, December 11, 2015, Homily for the Second Thursday of Advent, Priory of the Holy Spirit, Blackfriars, Oxford, https://www.godzdogz.op.org/godzdogz/is-john -the-baptist-elijah.

December 11: Third Sunday of Advent
Father Theophane Boyd, *Sundays at the Magic Monastery* (New York: Lantern Books, 2002), 20.

December 14:
Saint John of the Cross, Priest and Doctor of the Church
Gerard Manley Hopkins, "God's Grandeur" (1877).

Christine Valters Paintner, *Earth: Our Original Monastery* (Notre Dame, IN: Sorin Books, 2020), 22–23.

Paul Quenon, OCSO, *In Praise of a Useless Life: A Monk's Memoir* (Notre Dame, IN: Ave Maria Press, 2018), 42.

December 15: Thursday of the Third Week of Advent
St. Louis Jesuits, Songwriter Dan Schutte, "Though the Mountains May Fall" from *Earthen Vessels* (North American Liturgy Resources, 1975).

December 17: Saturday of the Third Week of Advent
Ann Voskamp, *How to Prepare for an Easy Advent*, https://ann voskamp.com/2015/11/how-to-prepare-for-an-easy-advent -when-the-first-snow-falls-quiet-on-the-trees-your-family -tree-feels-like-a-mess/.

December 21: Wednesday of the Fourth Week of Advent
Julian of Norwich, *The Revelations of Divine Love* (New York: Penguin Books, 1998), p. 85.

December 24: Saturday of the Fourth Week of Advent
(Christmas Eve)
Thomas Merton, *Thoughts in Solitude* (New York: Farrar, Straus and Giroux, 1956, 1958), 79.

December 25: The Nativity of the Lord (Christmas)
St. Benedict of Nursia, *The Rule of St. Benedict* (New York: Image Books, 1975), Prologue.

December 28: The Holy Innocents, Martyrs
Leonard Cohen, "Anthem," from *The Future* (Columbia Records, 1992).

December 31:
Seventh Day within the Octave of the Nativity of the Lord
U2, Songwriters Adam Clayton, Dave Evans, Larry Mullen, Paul Hewson, "Grace" from *All That You Can't Leave Behind* (Island/Interscope Records, 2000).
Catechism of the Catholic Church, 2nd ed. (United States Catholic Conference—Libreria Editrice Vaticana, 1997), 1996.

January 4: Saint Elizabeth Ann Seton, Religious
Dorothy Day, *Loaves and Fishes* (New York: Harper & Row, 1963).

January 8: The Epiphany of the Lord
Pope Francis, Epiphany homily, January 6, 2021, St. Peter's Basilica, https://www.vatican.va/content/francesco/en/homilies/2021/documents/papa-francesco_20210106_omelia-epifania.html.

January 9: The Baptism of the Lord
James Martin, SJ, *America Magazine*, January 14, 2019, https://www.americamagazine.org/faith/2019/01/14/james-martin-sj-why-was-jesus-baptized-232624.

SEASONAL REFLECTIONS NOW AVAILABLE IN ENGLISH AND SPANISH

LENT/CUARESMA

Not By Bread Alone: Daily Reflections for Lent 2023
Susan H. Swetnam

No sólo de pan: Reflexiones diarias para Cuaresma 2023
Susan H. Swetnam, translated by Luis Baudry Simón

EASTER/PASCUA

Rejoice and Be Glad:
Daily Reflections for Easter to Pentecost 2023
George M. Smiga and Ferdinand Okorie, CMF

Alégrense y regocíjense:
Reflexiones diarias de Pascua a Pentecostés 2023
George M. Smiga and Ferdinand Okorie, CMF,
translated by Luis Baudry Simón

ADVENT/ADVIENTO

Waiting in Joyful Hope:
Daily Reflections for Advent and Christmas 2023–2024
Susan H. Swetnam

Esperando con alegre esperanza:
Reflexiones diarias para Adviento y Navidad 2023–2024
Susan H. Swetnam, translated by Luis Baudry Simón

Standard, large-print, and eBook editions available. Call 800-858-5450 or visit www.litpress.org for more information and special bulk pricing discounts.

Ediciones estándar, de letra grande y de libro electrónico disponibles. Llame al 800-858-5450 o visite www.litpress.org para obtener más información y descuentos especiales de precios al por mayor.